Winston Churchill

Wendy Conklin, M.A.

Publishing Credits

Historical Consultant
Shannon C. McCutchen

Editor
Torrey Maloof

Editorial Director
Emily R. Smith, M.A.Ed.

Editor-in-Chief
Sharon Coan, M.S.Ed.

Creative Director
Lee Aucoin

Illustration Manager
Timothy J. Bradley

Publisher
Rachelle Cracchiolo, M.S.Ed.

Teacher Created Materials
5301 Oceanus Drive
Huntington Beach, CA 92649-1030
http://www.tcmpub.com
ISBN 978-0-7439-0669-2

Table of Contents

Churchill stands with his mother, Jennie Jerome.

This portrait shows Churchill as a young boy.

Churchill played a key role in World War II.

Who Was Winston Churchill?

Winston Churchill was born in 1874 into a very rich family. He grew up in Great Britain with his parents. He lived in a palace and had a duke for a grandfather.

Churchill died in 1965 at 90 years old. He led an exciting life. He once bravely escaped from a prisoner-of-war camp in South Africa. This event made him famous. He delivered more than 2,000 speeches in his life. In his spare time, he even painted. This amazing man served as Great Britain's prime minister two different times.

Just before the start of World War II, Churchill was 63 years old. Some British people felt he was a washed-up old man with nothing to offer. But, Churchill surprised the world with his leadership. This "washed-up old man" kept Adolf Hitler from taking over Europe.

Not a Good Test Taker

Churchill did not do very well when it came to taking tests. He had to take the army entrance test three times before he was finally admitted. This must have frustrated him.

V for Victory

Churchill encouraged the British people throughout the war. He formed his fingers like a V to stand for victory.

This sign has also been used in the United States to stand for "peace."

Churchill's Warnings

Germany lost World War I. The Treaty of Versailles (vuhr-SI) made Germans very angry. The cost of the war was just too much for them. France billed Germany billions of dollars for the war. The French blamed the Germans for ruining their land. Germany also lost 13 percent of its land. The seven million people who lived on this lost land were no longer called Germans. And, the treaty forced the German army to stay very small. The army could not have any tanks, planes, or submarines. Some people felt these **reparations** (reh-puh-RAY-shuhnz) were too severe.

Allies Caused Damage, Too

In truth, half of the World War I damage in France came from their allies. France should not have just blamed Germany for the losses.

Aryan Race

Adolf Hitler and other Nazis felt that the **Aryan** (AIR-ree-uhn) race was better than all others. The Aryans are the original speakers of the languages of Europe. Germans are Aryans. Nazis felt that Germans should rule all races.

This painting shows a model Nazi family. They are Aryans.

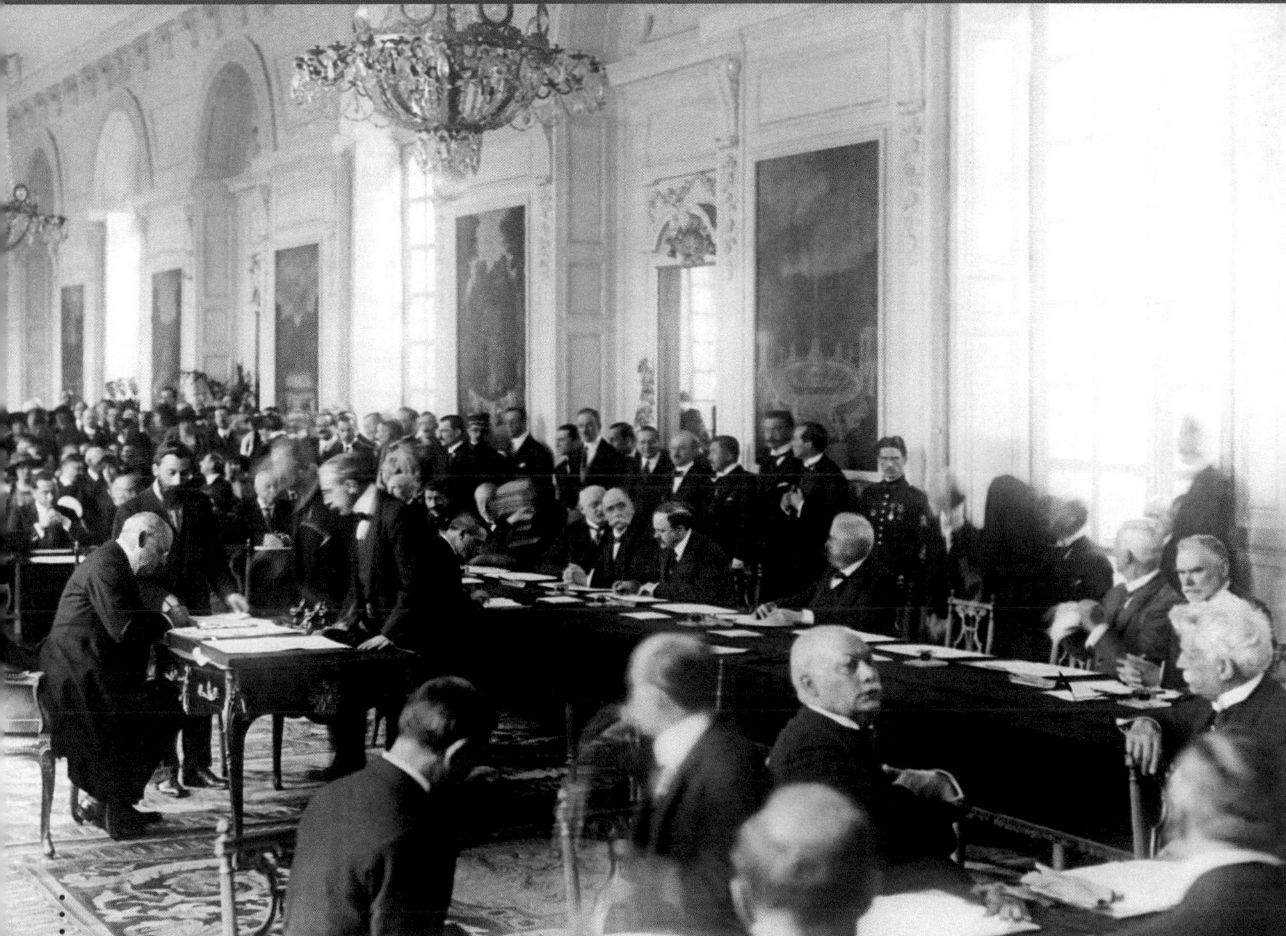

The Treaty of Versailles officially ended World War I. The treaty made Germans very angry.

Churchill was actively involved in World War I. At the end of the war, he predicted that the Treaty of Versailles would cause another war. Adolf Hitler was the leader of **Nazi** (NOT-see) Germany. Hitler was very angry about the Treaty of Versailles. When he rose to power in 1933, Churchill was worried. Hitler openly said that he was going to rebuild the German army. No one seemed to care except Churchill. Churchill wanted Great Britain to form a **pact** with France and the Soviet Union. He hoped the three countries would scare Hitler into backing down. Instead of listening, other people said that Churchill just wanted another war. They should have listened to him.

Churchill Was Right!

In 1938, Hitler announced a big plan. He merged his homeland of Austria with Germany. Great Britain's leader at the time was Neville Chamberlain. He just stepped aside and let Hitler take over Austria. But Churchill made speeches saying that Great Britain must prepare for war. He said, "And do not suppose that this is the end. This is only the beginning of the **reckoning** (REH-kuhn-ing)." Churchill realized that Hitler planned to continue taking over Europe.

Next, Hitler decided to take over Czechoslovakia (chek-uh-slow-VAW-kee-uh). He spread lies about how Germans were treated in the country. He also reminded Germans that Czechoslovakia was once part of Germany. It had been taken away after World War I.

At this point, Hitler met with Prime Minister Chamberlain. Germany and Great Britain agreed not go to war. The German army marched into Czechoslovakia with no shots fired.

Churchill was outraged. So were many other British people. It appeared that Great Britain would not stop Hitler.

Chamberlain did not like how Churchill was acting. But the British people were starting to listen to Churchill. Some of them felt he had been right all along.

This woman in Czechoslovakia is crying as the Nazis move into her country.

Pressure on the Austrian Jews

After Germans took over Austria, the Jewish people living there were treated differently. Signs warned Austrians not to buy from Jewish shop owners. This was just the beginning.

Nazi Symbol

In 1920, Hitler decided that the Nazis needed their own flag. On it, he placed the **swastika** (SWAWS-tih-kuh). This symbol was very old. It used to mean life, good luck, and power. Since the Nazis used the symbol, today it is seen as being very negative.

Prime Minister Chamberlain thought he could talk to Hitler and prevent another world war. He was wrong.

The Nazis put swastikas on flags, uniforms, and armbands.

Great Britain Goes to War

Hitler and the Germans wanted to take over more land. So Hitler planned to attack Poland. Prime Minister Chamberlain had said he would defend Poland. But, Hitler thought the British would give in like they had before.

There was still one threat in the way of Hitler taking over Poland. It was the Soviet leader, Joseph Stalin. Hitler sent

This Is Your Warning

Hitler hoped the quick defeat of Poland would scare Great Britain and France. He offered them a chance for peace, but they refused his offer. By this point, the leaders realized that they had to stop Hitler.

The Nazi Party

The German Nazi Party was **anti-Semitic** (an-tee-suh-MIH-tik). That means that they had strong feelings against Jewish people. The Nazi Party was a perfect fit for Hitler and his extreme views.

This Soviet poster reads, "We will achieve abundance!" It shows Joseph Stalin, the leader of the Soviet Union.

The Nazis treated Jewish people very badly. This banner outside of a Nazi headquarters reads, "By resisting the Jews, I fight for the Lord."

a secret telegram to Stalin. The telegram described the reasons Hitler thought Poland should be invaded. It blamed Poland for many problems. Hitler was offering to take care of a crisis. Hitler wrote that he wanted a new relationship with Stalin. He hoped that Stalin would support him. In just two days, Stalin told Hitler that he would not **interfere**. There was nothing stopping Hitler now.

On September 1, 1939, Hitler invaded Poland. This forced Great Britain to do something it did not want to do—declare war. World War II had officially begun.

Churchill's Destiny

Churchill could have said, "I told you so!" But, he did not. Instead, Churchill worked to strengthen the British Royal Navy. His leadership skills were clear. In May 1940, Chamberlain **resigned** (ruh-ZINED). Churchill became the new prime minister. Many British people believed he was the only one who could unite and lead the nation at war.

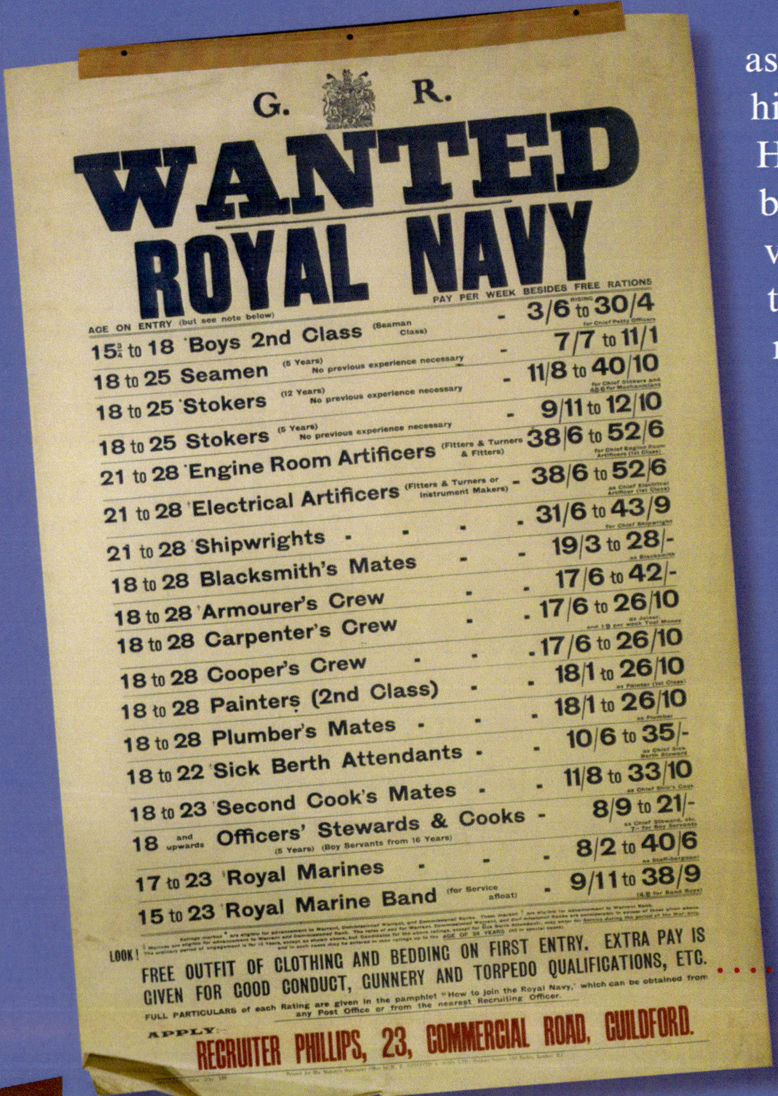

In World War II, the British Royal Navy operated almost 900 ships.

Churchill believed his job as Great Britain's leader was his **destiny** (DES-tuh-nee). He said, "My whole life has been building towards this very moment!" He believed that all his past experiences made him the right leader to fight Hitler.

Churchill had a way of calming people's fears. His speeches made people feel they could win the war. Even in the face of defeat, he rallied the British people. Those who did not like him in the past began to warm to him.

This is what it looks like out the bomb door of a plane. The puffs of smoke are bombs exploding or fighting on the ground.

A Funny Man!

There are many stories about Churchill's sense of humor. Once a woman was irritated with Churchill. She told him, "If you were my husband, I'd put poison in your coffee." Churchill replied, "If you were my wife, I'd drink it."

Famous Speech

After a defeat on the shores of France, Churchill said, "We shall fight on the beaches, we shall fight on the landing grounds, we shall fight in the fields and in the streets, we shall fight in the hills; we shall never **surrender** (suh-REN-duhr)!"

Churchill wanted to land with the British landing crews at Normandy. But, King George VI ordered him not to go.

Littering the Beach

When Hitler's troops arrived on the French beaches, they saw deserted British tanks and weapons all over. The British troops were saved, but their equipment was not. This victory made the Germans more confident than ever.

Hitler in Paris

The Germans took over Paris on June 14. There are many pictures of Hitler and the German army in Paris, France. As the capital, Paris represented the power of France. The fact that Hitler was at the Eiffel Tower was a crushing blow to the French people.

Hitler and his men visit the Eiffel Tower while Germany controlled Paris.

The Battle for France Ends

It was the spring of 1940. Churchill knew that Hitler's next move would be to conquer France. The British knew they had to help defend France against the Germans. British troops moved across the English Channel, which separates England from France. But, the British were not prepared to fight. German troops forced the British to **retreat** to the beaches.

Hitler ordered his tanks to stop their attack. When Hitler's troops arrived on the beaches days later, the British were gone. Churchill had rescued his men using rowboats and battleships. Even so, the Germans felt this was a great victory.

The French could not continue to fight the Germans by themselves. They **surrendered** to Germany on June 22. Now, all that stood in Hitler's way of controlling all of Europe was Churchill. Hitler offered Great Britain a deal. Churchill refused. He said, "The Battle of France is over. The Battle of Britain is about to begin."

These British soldiers are being taken prisoner by the Germans.

Leaders discuss the surrender of France to Germany.

The Battle of Britain

Hitler planned to send 160,000 soldiers across the English Channel. But he knew Churchill had a strong air force. So Hitler decided to destroy the British planes first. With the air force gone, he believed his troops could take over Great Britain easily.

The Germans used a strategy called **blitzkrieg** (BLITS-kreeg). This was a very fast and powerful way to fight. In this type of attack, planes begin by dropping bombs on the enemy. Then, the army moves in with tanks.

London suffered heavy damages during the battle.

The Germans began in August 1940 by bombing aircraft factories and planes. Then, night after night, the Germans dropped bombs on British cities.

Churchill told his people to turn out all their lights after sundown. This way, the bomber pilots would not know where the cities were located. Entire cities would disappear in the dark. The British built air-raid shelters underground. When alarms sounded, people rushed to these shelters. Even so, more than 40,000 British people died.

The British Royal Air Force (RAF) fought back. British fighter pilots fought Germans for control of the skies above Great Britain. The British refused to give up. By May 1941, Hitler realized he would not be able to beat the RAF. They were too strong and determined. So, Hitler gave up his plans to take control of Great Britain.

Children found safety in air-raid shelters during German bombing raids.

Aircraft spotters in London set off alarms. The alarms warned others when German planes were coming.

Never Forget the Pilots

Almost 3,000 British pilots fought in the Battle of Britain. It was the only World War II battle fought entirely in the air. The pilots had a dangerous job. The battle lasted almost four months. A total of 544 British pilots died. Their bravery stopped the Germans from taking over Great Britain.

Where's That Plane?

Plotters were young women who kept track of all the aircraft in the skies around Great Britain. They worked in secret underground rooms. These women received the locations of aircraft from different radar stations. Then, they plotted the locations of the planes. They did this by using long poles to push colored arrows around a large map on a table. The arrows represented the planes. These women had to move and think fast. By looking at the map, they could relay vital information to Great Britain's leaders and pilots.

Help from an Unlikely Friend

Churchill wanted to meet with the leader of the Soviet Union. Churchill hoped that Stalin would join the **Allied forces** even though he had joined sides with Hitler before the war began.

At the same time, Hitler was secretly making new plans. The German army was going to attack the Soviet Union. Hitler wanted a victory over the Soviets. That way, Churchill would think his last hope for help was gone. Some German officers thought this was a bad decision. But no one was willing to tell Hitler he was wrong.

Stalin was shocked at the German attack. He thought he had an agreement with Hitler. This was just what Churchill needed to get Stalin to switch to the Allies. Great Britain and the Soviet Union joined forces against Nazi Germany.

Hitler thought the Soviets would give up easily. But, the Germans could not win before winter arrived. The fighting continued the next spring. That fall, the Germans attacked Stalingrad (STAW-luhn-grad). Hitler's soldiers had no protection there. The Soviets surrounded the city and trapped Hitler's men.

Allies vs. Axis Powers

There were two sides in World War II. Germany, Italy, and Japan were on one side. They were known as the **Axis powers**. On the other side were Great Britain, France, and the Soviet Union. Together, these countries were known as the Allies. The United States joined the Allies later in the war.

Stalingrad Prisoners

At Stalingrad, 91,000 German men surrendered to the Soviets. As many as 85,000 of them died in Soviet prison camps.

This medal was awarded to all soldiers in the Soviet armed forces.

Churchill visited Moscow, Russia, in August 1942. There, he met Joseph Stalin for the first time.

German prisoners of war are being led through Stalingrad in 1943.

Roosevelt to the Rescue!

Churchill knew he needed more help to defeat Hitler. So, he started secret talks with the United States president, Franklin D. Roosevelt.

President Roosevelt had promised Americans that he would not enter the war unless attacked. On December 7, 1941, Japan carried out a secret attack. It was at a U.S. military base in Hawaii. The base was called Pearl Harbor. The United States had battleships and other military ships and planes there.

Around 8:00 A.M., hundreds of Japanese planes started bombing the base. Their bombs blew some of the U.S. battleships in half. Fire and smoke spread quickly. More than 2,400 Americans died that day. The next day, Roosevelt asked Congress to declare war on Japan. He told the country, "Yesterday is a day that will live in **infamy** (IN-fuh-mee)!"

The USS *Arizona* burns at Pearl Harbor, December 7, 1941.

Roosevelt's Fight

Roosevelt wanted to go to war, but others did not agree. Some people thought the United States should be a good example of peace. Other people believed that the United States should only worry about itself.

Roosevelt Needs Support

To join the war, Roosevelt needed the support of the people. He got it in December 1941. Pearl Harbor made Americans angry. They were ready to fight back.

President Roosevelt asks Congress for a declaration of war against Japan on December 8, 1941.

President Roosevelt is seated with Churchill at the White House.

The Next Steps

Life for Jewish people throughout Europe was very hard during the war. At first, they were forced to live in **ghettos** (GET-toez). Ghettos were very crowded and dirty. There was little food. Many people died of starvation and disease.

Next, the Nazis began to move the Jewish people to **concentration** (kon-suhn-TRAY-shun) **camps**. Living there was even harder than in the ghettos. Prisoners had to work to survive. The work was hard and people were given little to eat. Some of these camps were death camps where millions of people were killed.

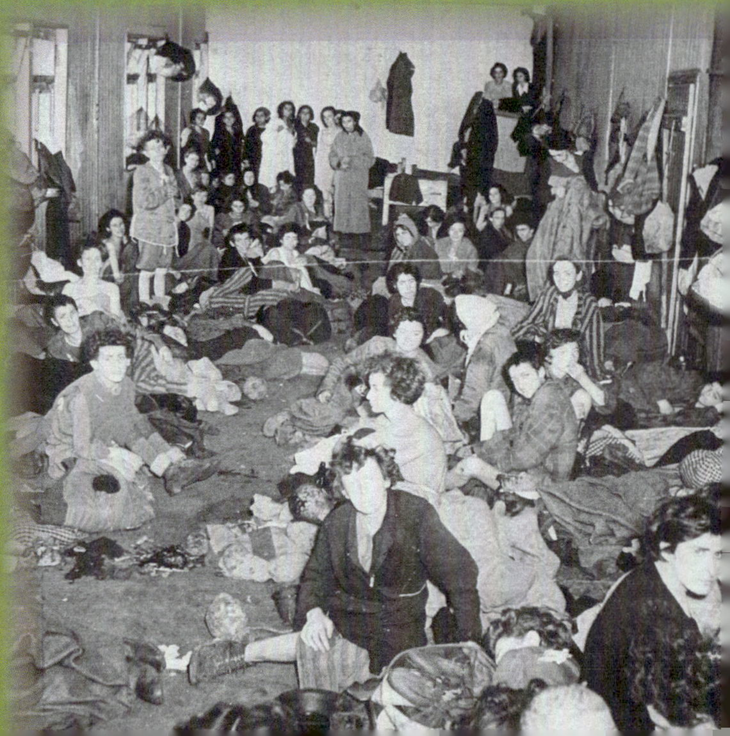

Words from Hitler

"The greater the lie, the greater the chance that it will be believed." In other words, crowds often fall for big lies, not small ones. These words came from a man who told some pretty big lies, Adolf Hitler.

Hitler's Friends

Hitler looked to a few powerful friends to help him win the war. He formed an **alliance** (uh-LIE-untz) with Benito Mussolini (buh-NEE-tow moos-soh-LEE-nee), the leader of Italy. Hitler also made an agreement with the emperor of Japan.

Benito Mussolini led Italy during World War II.

This sign is part of a former Nazi concentration camp. The sign reads, "Work will set you free."

In December 1941, World War II changed. The United States declared war on Japan. Three days later, Germany and Italy declared war on the United States. However, it would still be more than three years before the war ended. During these three years, the Jewish people of Europe continued to suffer and be murdered.

The United States fought two wars. Forces were sent to Europe to fight the Germans. Other troops traveled by ship to the Pacific to fight Japan. Churchill had new hope that the Allies could defeat Germany.

The Allies needed to take back France. In June 1944, the Allies stormed the beaches at Normandy, France. The Allied troops started moving across France. The Germans fled in front of them. People around the world thought the war was coming to an end. The Germans could not continue to fight. The Allies were just too powerful now. The British people saw an end to the long war.

These women and children are being detained in a concentration camp.

The End of the War

The Allies sent bomber planes over German cities. For the first time in the war, Germany was under attack. This time, the Germans were the ones hiding in shelters. The British and Americans were in the air.

Hitler told his people to defend their capital city, Berlin. But, it was too late. Soviet forces entered Berlin in April 1945. By this time, the Soviets had lost about 20 million people. They wanted to punish the Germans for the war.

The Soviets found Hitler's underground **bunker**, but it was too late. Hitler could not face a surrender. So he killed himself before they found him. The war in Europe was finally over in May 1945.

The Allies found the terrible concentration camps. There were starving people and dead bodies all over these camps.

One part of the war may have ended, but another part was still going strong. The war in the Pacific still had four months of bloody battles. And, leaders of Japan and the United States had important decisions to make.

Experts examine Hitler's bunker. The bunker contained about 30 small underground rooms.

Hitler was a powerful and persuasive speaker.

Who Would Believe Hitler?

When the German people heard Hitler speak, they felt that he could take away their problems. He promised them jobs and dignity. Life was hard. The Germans needed hope. They thought Hitler gave this to them. In the end, he only brought them shame.

May 8, 1945

Churchill gave a speech on this day. He said, "We may allow ourselves a brief period of rejoicing; but let us not forget for a moment the toil and efforts that lie ahead. Japan with all her **treachery** (TREH-chuh-ree) and greed, remains **unsubdued** (un-sub-DEWD)."

This is a group of German prisoners of war after the fall of the German army.

Hirohito is crowned emperor of Japan.

Hirohito, the empress, and President Ford

Hirohito Visits the United States

In 1975, Hirohito visited the United States. He met actor John Wayne and President Gerald Ford. He even bought and wore a Mickey Mouse watch!

A Marine Biologist

Hirohito studied marine biology. He enjoyed classifying sea animals and plants. He did this even when he was emperor of Japan.

Other World War II Leaders

Winston Churchill's leadership was very important during World War II. Great Britain and the Allies won the war. There were other leaders during the war who helped change the world. President Roosevelt was one of them. The following pages describe two other powerful leaders.

A Wartime God-King

There are some leaders who always find themselves in a war. Japan had one of these emperors. His name was Hirohito (hear-oh-HEE-tow). He led Japan from 1926 to 1989. In 1937, his country went to war with China. Just a few years later, he joined World War II.

At the time, people thought of Hirohito as a peaceful man. They believed that his military leaders made all the decisions. That was not true. He knew about Pearl Harbor. He even gave tips on how to carry out the attack. And, he chose to form an alliance with Germany and Italy.

Japan lost about three million people during World War II. Hirohito knew he had to surrender. In 1945, he spoke to his people over the radio. It was the first time the country heard his voice. He never used the word *surrender*, but his message was clear. Japan must stop fighting the war.

Hirohito made a deal with the United States. He promised to get his people to support peace with the United States. In return, Hirohito did not have to stand trial for his part in the war.

Emperor Hirohito in 1918

Other World War II Leaders *(cont.)*

A True Man

Harry S. Truman was Roosevelt's third vice president. He took office in 1945. He did not see much of Roosevelt in his first few weeks in office. Shortly after, President Roosevelt died. After Roosevelt's death, Truman found himself in charge of a war. Truman did not know that the United States had an **atomic bomb**. Needless to say, Truman learned a lot when he became president.

As the new president, Truman faced a big decision: Should he drop the atomic bomb on Japan? And if he did, where should it be dropped?

The United States had two of these superbombs. First, Truman asked Japan to surrender. The Japanese refused. Truman knew he had to end the war. Thousands of U.S. soldiers were dying. So, he decided to drop the bomb. He hoped the Japanese would give up after seeing one of their cities destroyed.

On August 6, 1945, the United States dropped an atomic bomb on Hiroshima (huh-ROW-shuh-muh). Truman picked that place because Japan's army trained there. Three days later, another bomb was dropped on Nagasaki (nah-gah-SAH-kee). The Japanese knew they were beaten. They surrendered. The war was finally over.

On April 15, 1945, Truman spoke to Congress. He said that the United States would not stop fighting until Germany and Japan surrendered.

This is the cloud produced by the atomic bomb dropped on Nagasaki, Japan.

When an Atomic Bomb Drops

What does an atomic bomb do when it is dropped? Its shock wave makes everything in its path disappear. Its **thermal** (THUHR-muhl) rays burn people. Fire burns in all directions, and thick dust covers the sky.

Effects of Radiation

Hundreds of thousands of Japanese people died in the years after the bombs were dropped. **Radiation** (ray-dee-AY-shuhn) from the blasts made them sick.

There are all kinds of leaders in the world. Some leaders inspire hope in others. Some leaders only bring pain. Winston Chuchill was a man who inspired Great Britain. He supported the British people as they fought against a powerful enemy. Without him, the outcome of World War II would have been very different.

Glossary

alliance—agreement to fight with one another; a friendship between countries

Allied forces—Great Britain, France, the Soviet Union, and the United States

anti-Semitic—to be against Semitic people; the Jewish population is one of these groups

Aryan—the original speakers of the European languages, including the Germans

atomic bomb—a bomb made from the splitting of atoms

Axis powers—Germany, Japan, and Italy

blitzkrieg—a battle strategy where planes drop many bombs in a surprise attack on an enemy before tanks attack

bunker—an underground shelter

concentration camps—camps where people are contained; similar to prisons

destiny—planned to be, as if a greater force made it happen

ghettos—overcrowded slums where many people live in small areas

infamy—made famous because of an evil deed

interfere—to get in the way or stop

Nazi—political party that controlled Germany from 1933–1945

pact—an agreement

radiation—energy waves from a nuclear weapon

reckoning—settling debts; paying for crimes that have been committed

reparations—punishments and payments for something

resigned—to have given up one's position or responsibilities

retreat—to back away from the battle

surrendered—stopped fighting

swastika—symbol that represented the Nazi Party

thermal—a rising column of air caused by heat

treachery—breaking agreements

unsubdued—unstopped; still going

Index

Image Credits

cover The Granger Collection, New York; p.1 The Granger Collection, New York; p.4 (top) The Library of Congress; p.4 (bottom left) The Library of Congress; p.4 (bottom right) The Library of Congress; p.5 Blaz Kure/Shutterstock, Inc.; p.6 The Granger Collection, New York; p.7 Underwood & Underwood/Corbis; p.8 The Library of Congress; p.9 (top) Corbis; p.9 (bottom) ullstein bild/The Granger Collection, New York; p.10 The Granger Collection, New York; p.11 Hulton-Deutsch Collection/Corbis; p.12 The Library of Congress; p.13 (top) The Library of Congress; p.13 (bottom) Hulton Archive/Getty Images; p.14 Corbis; p.15 (top) The Granger Collection, New York; p.15 (bottom) The National Archives; p.16 Corbis; p.17 (top) The Library of Congress; p.17 (bottom) Corbis; p.18 Uss Sergey Valentinovich/Shutterstock, Inc.; p.19 (top) The Library of Congress; p.19 (bottom) The Granger Collection, New York; p.20 The Granger Collection, New York; p.21 (top) Corbis; p.21 (bottom) The Granger Collection, New York; p.22 (left) The Library of Congress; p.22 (right) Bettmann/Corbis; p.23 Ira Nowinski/Corbis; p.24 Bettmann/Corbis; p.25 (top) Photos.com; p.25 (bottom) The Library of Congress; p.26 (left) Wally McNamee/Corbis; p.26 (right) The Library of Congress; p.27 The Library of Congress; p.28–29 The Library of Congress; p.29 Corbis